Early
SCIENCE
Encyclopedias

BIOMES

by A. W. Buckey

Early Encyclopedias

An Imprint of Abdo Reference
abdobooks.com

abdobooks.com

Published by Abdo Reference, a division of ABDO, PO Box 398166, Minneapolis, Minnesota 55439.

Printed in China.
052024
092024

THIS BOOK CONTAINS RECYCLED MATERIALS

Editor: Marie Pearson
Series Designers: Candice Keimig, Joshua Olson
Production Designers: Ryan Gale, Joshua Olson

Library of Congress Control Number: 2023949354

Publisher's Cataloging-in-Publication Data

Names: Buckey, A. W., author.
Title: Biomes / by A. W. Buckey
Description: Minneapolis, Minnesota: Abdo Reference, 2025 | Series: Early science encyclopedias | Includes online resources and index.
Identifiers: ISBN 9781098294243 (lib. bdg.) | ISBN 9798384913511 (ebook)
Subjects: LCSH: Biotic communities--Juvenile literature. | Habitat (Ecology)--Juvenile literature. | Ecology--Juvenile literature. | Biodiversity--Juvenile literature. | Science--Juvenile literature. | Encyclopedias and dictionaries--Juvenile literature.
Classification: DDC 577.0--dc23

CONTENTS

INTRODUCTION

Coral reefs are home to many species of fish, corals, and other living things.

Living Together

Earth is full of life. Plants and animals live in environments called biomes. *Bios* is the Greek word for "life." Biomes are places where many kinds of life come together. All biomes are different. Some have hot weather. Others are cold. Some are on land. Others are in the water.

Things in Common

Biomes have a few things in common. They are all important parts of the natural world. Climate change and pollution can harm biomes. But people are working to protect these wonderful places.

People plant trees to give animals food and shelter.

What Is a Desert?

Deserts are dry. They get less than 10 inches (25 cm) of rain each year. These biomes tend to be hot during the day. Sand and rocks reflect the sun's heat. This warms the air near the ground.

People may picture deserts as having few plants. But most have some plants.

Night Temperature

At night, deserts usually get cold. That is because the air is dry. Humid air, or air with water, traps heat. Dry air traps less heat. After dark, the ground has no more heat to reflect. The heat rises and spreads high in the air. This leaves the desert cool.

DESERT BIOMES

Location

There are deserts on all seven continents. There are different kinds of desert biomes. They have different temperatures.

Types

Hot deserts are very hot during the day. They are cooler at night. Semiarid deserts are not as hot as hot deserts. Mountains may block rain from these deserts. Coastal deserts are near the sea. They are cooler than semiarid deserts. Cold deserts have long winters. They stay frozen for much of the year.

FUN FACT!

The Sahara Desert in Africa is about as big as the United States.

Desert Summer Temperatures

	Average High	Average Low
Hot desert: Sonoran Desert	98 degrees Fahrenheit (37°C)	74 degrees Fahrenheit (23°C)
Semiarid desert: Gobi Desert	86 degrees Fahrenheit (30°C)	48 degrees Fahrenheit (9°C)
Coastal desert: Atacama Desert	75 degrees Fahrenheit (24°C)	42 degrees Fahrenheit (6°C)
Cold desert: Antarctica (South Pole)	–15 degrees Fahrenheit (–26°C)	–20 degrees Fahrenheit (–29°C)

Desert Plants

Plants need water to stay alive. Surviving on little water can be hard. There are fewer plants in deserts than in many other biomes. But desert plants have ways to live on little water. They also protect themselves from desert dangers such as heat.

Cacti

A cactus is a desert plant. Cacti have flowers. They store water in their stems. Cacti grow spines. Spines protect water in a cactus from thirsty animals. Spines also make small shadows on the cactus. They help keep the plant cool.

All but one species of cacti are native to the Americas.

Saguaros

A saguaro is a species of cactus. It grows in the Sonoran Desert. This desert is in the southwestern United States and part of Mexico. Saguaros can grow up to 60 feet (18 m) tall. They have branches that look like arms.

FUN FACT!

The saguaro can hold about 1,000 gallons (3,800 L) of water inside its long stem.

The saguaro can live for about 200 years.

Other Plants

There are few trees in deserts. Many desert plants are shrubs. Shrubs are short with many stems.

Yuccas

Some desert shrubs are yuccas. There are about 40 species of yuccas. They live in North American deserts. Yuccas have long leaves shaped like swords. These plants are succulents. This means that their thick leaves store water.

Antarctic Plants

The cold Antarctic desert is a tough place for plants. But the Antarctic pearlwort lives there. It has bright yellow flowers. The pearlwort is one of only two kinds of Antarctic plants with roots, leaves, and stems. The other species is a grass called hair grass.

Pearlwort is most common in rocky coastal areas of Antarctica.

Desert Animals

Desert animals also deal with the heat and lack of water. They have adapted to desert biomes. Their bodies store water. They have ways of hiding from the heat.

The Arabian oryx can get much of the water it needs from its food.

Camels have padded, two-toed feet.

Camels

Camels live in Africa and Asia. Their humps are full of fat. When camels cannot find food, their bodies use this fat for energy. Camels can also go up to ten months without drinking water. They can walk long distances. Their big feet are shaped like snowshoes. This helps them balance on desert sands.

Camels

People in deserts sometimes use camels to carry things. The strongest camels can carry more than 400 pounds (180 kg).

Kangaroos

In Australia, kangaroos lick their arms to cool off. The water from their spit dries in the air. This causes heat to leave the kangaroos' bodies.

Like kangaroos, wallabies lick their arms to keep cool.

Coyotes

Coyotes are predators that sometimes live in deserts. They live in North and Central America. Coyotes eat all kinds of animals. They will also eat prey that is already dead. Desert food can be hard to find. Eating a variety of things helps coyotes survive.

Reptiles

Some desert animals use the environment to warm up or cool down. Desert reptiles burrow into the cool ground to cool off. And they have ways to find water. The thorny devil is an Australian lizard. The scales on its back help water trickle to its mouth.

The thorny devil eats ants.

Birds

Many desert birds travel far to find food and water. The cactus wren lives in American and Mexican deserts. These spotted birds make their nests inside cacti. The holes to their nests let cool winds blow inside.

Scorpions live on all continents except Antarctica.

Scorpions

Scorpions live in many deserts. They have pincers and a stinging tail. The venom inside the tail kills prey. The bark scorpion lives in deserts in Arizona, California, and Mexico. It hunts in the cool of night.

Protecting Deserts

Because of climate change, Earth is getting hotter. Climate change is happening faster in deserts than in other places. This is because deserts heat up more quickly.

Bare ground dries out more quickly than ground covered in plants because it is more exposed to sunlight and wind.

Heat

More heat can dry up water. This can be deadly to plants and animals. Scientists are working to protect desert plants and animals. They study how hotter temperatures could affect desert life.

When plants die, desert animals lose their food sources.

People in Mongolia plant desert shrubs to protect the ground from becoming too dry.

Replanting

Clearing land for farming or building roads damages deserts. Plants may disappear. The plants in deserts support animals and soil. Wildlife cannot thrive without plants. Some people grow and plant desert species to help deserts recover.

Biocrust

Many deserts are covered with a biocrust. This is a layer of small life-forms. A biocrust is like glue. It keeps soil from blowing away.

What Is a Forest?

A forest biome has many trees close together. Trees are usually tall plants. Most have just one stem, or trunk. Branches grow from the trunk. Leaves grow on the branches. The trunks and branches are made of wood.

Canopies

The top of a tree is called its crown. Together, these crowns are called a forest canopy. Sometimes canopies are very thick. The tree crowns touch each other.

FUN FACT!

The oldest tree in the world lives in California. Its name is Methuselah. It is almost 5,000 years old.

A forest canopy may or may not let sunlight through to the ground.

Tree Height

Adult trees tend to be taller than 16 feet (5 m). The tallest tree in the world is a coast redwood in California. It is called Hyperion. It stands almost 380 feet (116 m) tall.

Rainforest Layers

Different animals are suited for different layers of the rainforest.

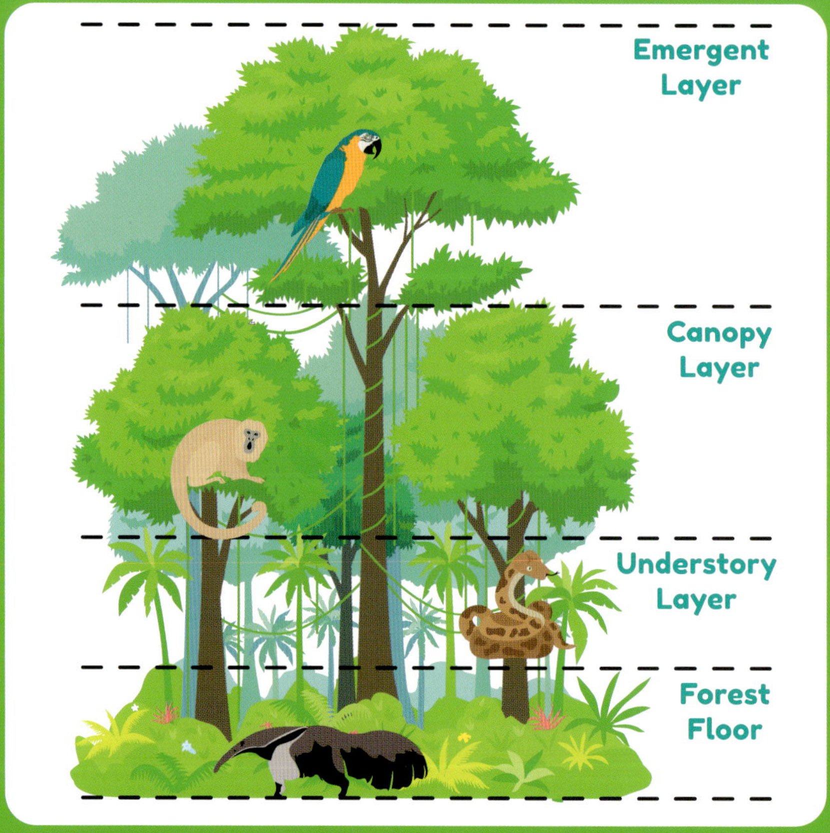

Tropical Rainforests

All continents except Antarctica have forests. There are three main types of forests. They have different weather and types of trees. Tropical rainforests are near the equator. The equator is the imaginary line around the middle of Earth. This region is warm year-round. Tropical rainforests have thick canopies. Little sunlight reaches below.

In autumn, the leaves on deciduous trees turn bright colors before falling.

Temperate Forests

Temperate forests are farther from the equator. They have four seasons. The leaves on many trees here grow in warm weather. They fall off in cold weather. Trees with leaves that fall are called deciduous.

Boreal Forests

Boreal forests are in the far north. It is cold there. Trees there are usually conifers. These are trees with cones. Boreal forests cover more land than any other biome.

Pine cone

Another name for boreal forests is taiga.

Forest Plants

The forest is full of trees. Seeds must spread away from parent trees. This way adult trees do not take all the water and sunlight from young trees.

A maple tree seed has a wing that causes it to spin away from the tree as it falls.

A durian fruit is the size of a watermelon.

Durian Tree

The durian tree grows in Asia's tropical rainforests. This tree can grow up to 165 feet (50 m) tall. Durian trees have spiky fruit called durians. The fruit has a very strong smell. Large animals such as elephants eat durians. The elephants move around, and the seeds are passed in the animals' poop. The seeds end up away from the parent tree.

FUN FACT!

In some countries, people cannot bring a durian fruit on a train or bus. This is because the fruit's smell is so strong.

Orchid roots wrap around the tree it grows on.

Orchids

Tropical rainforests are home to other plants too. Orchids are plants with colorful flowers. Most grow on the branches of other plants. Butterflies and bees eat nectar from orchids. They spread pollen from one flower to another. This helps the flowers make seeds.

Evergreens

Many conifer trees are evergreen. An evergreen tree does not lose its leaves with the seasons. This is helpful in winter, when it is darker than in summer. Plants need sunlight to get energy. Making new leaves takes a lot of energy.

Spruce trees are evergreens that are often shaped like a triangle.

Evergreen Features

Most evergreens have needle-shaped leaves. The needles are coated in wax. This helps limit water loss. Douglas firs, Fraser firs, and white pines are all conifers.

The longest pine needles grow up to 1.5 feet (0.5 m) long.

The rough cocklebur seed has hooked spikes that catch in animals' fur.

Forest Animals

The forest is a diverse place. Animals take shelter in wooded areas. Animals help the forest grow by spreading seeds. Some forest animals hunt prey.

Small Mammals

Forests are home to many small mammals. Squirrels and bats live in the trees. Shrews and rabbits live on forest floors.

Moose

There are also large mammals. Moose are the biggest members of the deer family. They live in northern Europe, Asia, and North America. Moose eat tree leaves and bark. They are good swimmers. They can eat the plants in ponds.

Gorillas

The gorilla is a tropical rainforest mammal from Africa. Gorillas are primates. This group also includes chimpanzees and humans. Gorillas live in families. They travel together. They eat mostly fruits and plant stems. Their forest home has a lot of these foods.

There are fewer than 150,000 wild western lowland gorillas.

Birds

More birds live in forests than in any other biome. They eat the plants and animals that live there. After eating fruit, birds spread seeds through their droppings. Brightly colored macaws fly through tropical rainforests in the Americas. Macaws' strong beaks help them crack open hard seeds.

The scarlet macaw is up to 2.8 feet (0.9 m) long from beak to tail.

A parrot's beak is always growing, like a fingernail. Eating nuts keeps the beak short.

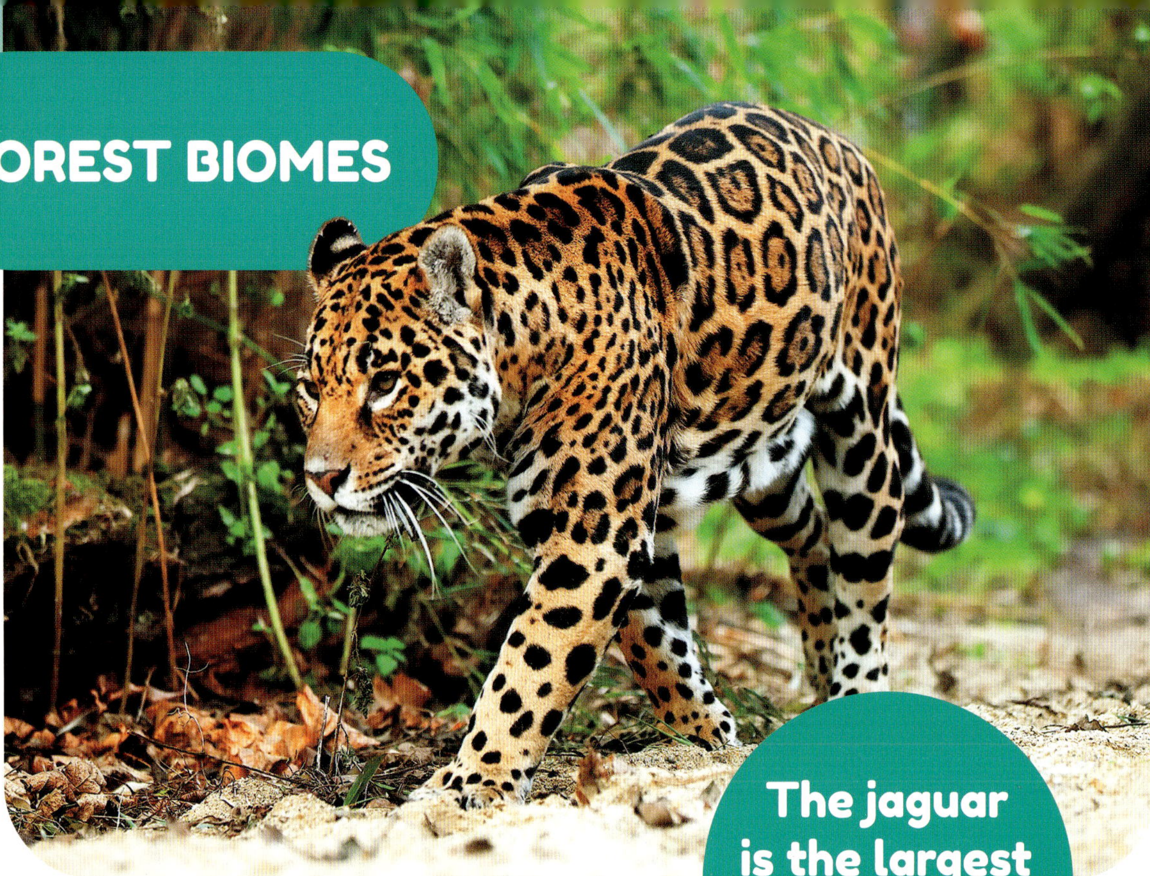

The jaguar is the largest cat in the Americas.

Jaguars

The jaguar is a large rainforest cat. It lives in South and Central America. Jaguars' sharp, curved claws help them climb trees. Sometimes they hunt from trees. Their spots help them blend in with the spots of light shining through the treetops.

Black Bears

Black bears live in forests in North America. They stay in dens during the winter. They live off of stored fat.

Tree Frogs

Tree frogs are forest amphibians. In South America, colorful tree frogs live in the rainforest. They have sticky pads on their toes. The pads help them climb plants.

Poison Dart Frogs

The poison dart frog has a deadly toxin in its skin. Some people use this poison to hunt.

The white-lipped tree frog is the biggest tree frog. It grows up to 5 inches (13 cm) long.

Protecting Forests

Forests have an important job. Trees take a gas called carbon dioxide from the air. This helps keep the planet from getting too warm. Some scientists call forests Earth's air conditioner.

A tree's leaves take in carbon dioxide.

Replanting

Many forests are cut down to make land for farms. This leaves fewer trees to help cool Earth. Some people are regrowing forests. The United Nations is a world organization. It is trying to replant forests around the world.

What Are Freshwater Biomes?

Fresh water is water that is not salty. It has less than 1 percent salt. Seawater has about 3.5 percent salt. Water that is between 1 percent and 3.5 percent is called brackish.

Types

Freshwater biomes are on all continents. They are in and around bodies of fresh water. Lakes, rivers, ponds, springs, and streams are all fresh water.

People enjoy canoeing on lakes.

These biomes have different life-forms. But they also have plants and animals in common.

Estuaries

Estuaries are places where rivers meet the sea. They are a mix of fresh water and salt water.

Freshwater Bodies

LAKE

A body of water surrounded by land. Usually deeper and bigger than a pond.

POND

A body of water surrounded by land. Sunlight can reach the bottom of a pond.

RIVER

A large, flowing freshwater body.

STREAM

A flowing freshwater body that is narrower than a river.

FRESHWATER BIOMES

A lily pad's leaf can hold small frogs.

Plants

Freshwater biomes are wet and muddy. The plants that live there grow in and around water. They anchor in the soil to stay in place.

Water Lilies

Some plants grow on top of water. The water lily is a freshwater flower. Water lilies grow from the bottom of a freshwater body. Their stems rise from the water. The water lily grows a leaf called a pad on top of the water. Each plant has one flower.

FUN FACT!

Lotus plants are a Buddhist symbol. The flower blooms in muddy water. This is an example of how good things can come from hard times.

Lotus flowers are similar to water lilies. But they bloom higher above the water.

Reeds

Reeds are tall grasses. They grow on the edges of freshwater bodies. Reeds make homes for animals alongside the water. They also help keep the soil from washing away.

Cattails are a common reed near shorelines.

Some algae cling to rocks.

Algae

Many rivers and streams have green, slimy life-forms on rocks. These are freshwater algae. Algae are simple life-forms. Most have just one cell. They help make oxygen. They clean the water. Small animals eat them.

FUN FACT!

Ancient Egyptians made the first paper about 5,000 years ago. They made it with a reed called papyrus from the Nile River.

Freshwater Animals

Freshwater biomes are home to many animals. These animals often have special ways of breathing. They find food in the water.

Fish

Fish have gills that let them breathe underwater. Catfish live at the bottoms of lakes and rivers. These fish have barbels on their heads. The barbels look like a cat's whiskers. They help the catfish taste. Catfish have good taste, sight, and hearing. They can find food to eat in the mud.

Piranhas

The piranha is a fish in South American rivers. Some eat meat. They have sharp teeth. These fish hunt in groups. When one fish finds prey, the rest of the group gathers. A group of piranhas can work together to kill large prey.

There are more than 60 species of piranhas.

Wetlands and other freshwater bodies in Asia are home to the smooth-coated otter.

Breathing Air

Many other freshwater animals breathe air. They can hold their breath a long time. This helps them hunt underwater.

Dolphins

River dolphins live in South America and Asia. South America has the pink Amazon river dolphin and the tucuxi. There are a few kinds of Asian river dolphins.

Dolphin Traits

Many rivers are muddy. It is hard to see in the water. River dolphins hunt and travel with echolocation. This means they use sound to tell where things are.

Breathing

Dolphins breathe air. A dolphin gets air through a blowhole on the top of its head. It closes the blowhole when it is underwater.

The Amazon river dolphin usually swims at about 1 to 2 miles per hour (1.6 to 3.2 kmh).

Amazon River dolphins do not dive deep. They breathe every 30 seconds to two minutes.
blowhole

Alligators have about 80 teeth.

Alligators

Alligators are large freshwater reptiles. American alligators grow to be 10 to 15 feet (3 to 4.6 m) long. They can weigh up to 1,000 pounds (450 kg). An alligator's strong tail helps it swim.

Caimans

Caimans are reptiles in the alligator family. They live in Central America, Mexico, and South America. Most are smaller than alligators.

Breathing

The alligator can close its throat underwater. This keeps it from swallowing water when catching prey. An alligator usually takes a breath of air every 20 to 30 minutes.

An alligator's eyes are on the top of its head so it can stay mostly hidden underwater while hunting.

Bullfrogs

Most amphibians spend part of their lives in fresh water and part on land. American bullfrog tadpoles hatch from eggs. They live in fresh water. They breathe with gills. They swim with tails.

Growing Up

As tadpoles age, they grow legs. The tail and gills disappear. They breathe air. Adults can hop on land and swim in water.

The American bullfrog can stay in tadpole form for up to 3 years.

American bullfrogs are about as long as an adult's hand.

Ibises

Some birds hunt in rivers and lakes. The ibis is a freshwater bird. It has long legs and a long bill. It walks through shallow water to look for fish or mussels. Ibises live all over the world.

The white-faced ibis is mostly purple, green, and bronze in color.

Herons

Herons are also long-legged wading birds. Their long toes help them balance in the mud. They wait until prey is close. Then the birds grab the fish with their bills.

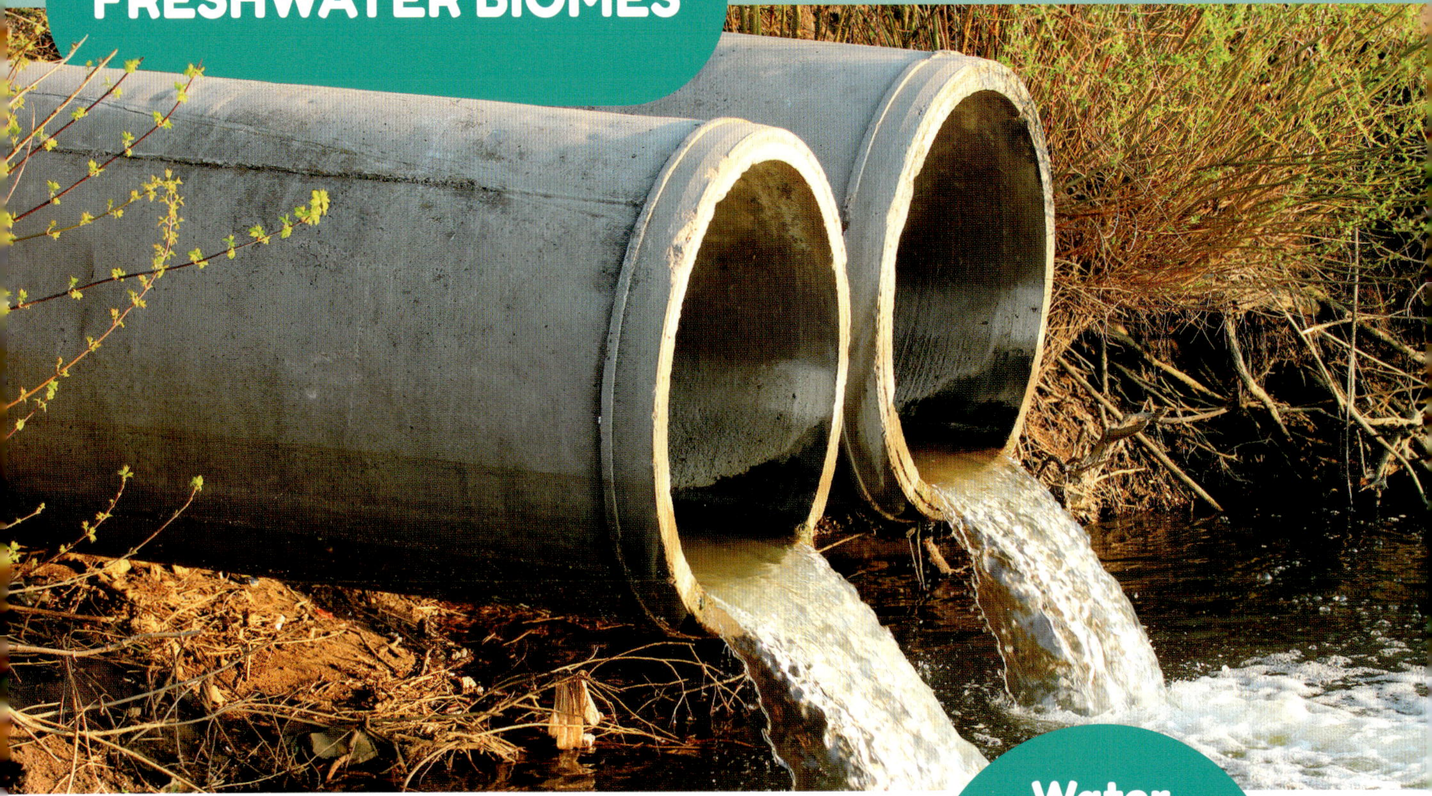

Water pollution can come from human waste.

Protecting Freshwater Biomes

Only 3 percent of Earth's water is fresh. Many plants and animals, including humans, need this water to live. Fresh water can become polluted. This is when chemicals and objects enter the water. They make the water unsafe to drink. Pollution can make animals such as frogs unable to lay eggs.

Clean Water

People are working to clean fresh water. For example, the Ganges River in India is polluted. The Indian government is building facilities that can clean the water.

People work together to clean Ruaka River in Kenya.

What Are Grasslands?

A grassland is a biome covered mostly in grass. Grasslands tend to be dry. There is not enough water for most trees. Grasslands are on every continent except Antarctica.

FUN FACT!

The African bush elephant lives in the savanna. It is the world's biggest land mammal. These elephants eat about 350 pounds (160 kg) of grass and other foods a day.

Grasslands are windy because there are so few trees and hills to block the wind.

Acacia trees are found in African and Australian savannas.

Savannas

There are two main types of grasslands. Savannas have rainy and dry seasons. They are warm all year and have a few scattered trees. Savannas are common in Africa. There are also large savannas in Australia and South America.

Different species of wildflowers in prairies bloom during different seasons.

Temperate Grasslands

Temperate grasslands are the other type of grasslands. These have hot and cold weather. They usually do not have shrubs or trees. Prairies in the United States are temperate grasslands.

Grasses

Many grasses survive in the dry soil of grasslands. The plants in grasslands are food for animals. They support life in the biome.

Wild mustangs are among the animals that eat grasses.

Rhodes Grass

Rhodes grass grows in southern African savannas. It can grow more than 6 feet (1.8 m) tall. This grass can survive a long dry season. Animals eat Rhodes grass.

Rhodes grass grows tufts of seeds.

Switchgrass stays upright year-round.

Switchgrass

Switchgrass is an American prairie grass. It grows up to 5 feet (1.5 m) tall. Switchgrass has very deep roots. The roots help it find water in dry soil.

Insects such as bees eat the nectar and pollen of the purple prairie clover.

Flowers

Some grassland plants have colorful flowers. The purple prairie clover grows in North American grasslands. In summer, it grows purple flowers. Many prairie animals eat clover. This plant is high in protein. Animals need protein in food.

Trees

Grasslands have few trees. One exception is the baobab. Baobabs grow in Africa and Australia. They have thick trunks and small branches. Grassland animals live in the branches. They can also eat the tree's fruit and nectar.

Baobabs store water in their thick trunks.

Grassland Animals

Many grassland animals survive on grasses. American bison are large North American mammals. Bison eat mostly grasses. A bison can eat more than 30 pounds (14 kg) of grass a day.

Hunting Bison

There used to be millions of bison in North America. Many were killed by sport hunters.

American bison have thick coats to keep them warm in cold winters.

Prairie dogs live in groups called colonies. Their tunnel systems can be large.

Prairie Dogs

The prairie dog lives in North American grasslands. Prairie dogs are rodents. There are few hiding places in grasslands. So prairie dogs make tunnel systems called burrows. They hide from predators in the burrows. They also take shelter from the weather in them.

Prairie Dog Colony

The biggest prairie dog colony covered 25,000 square miles (65,000 sq km). That is bigger than the state of West Virginia.

Giraffes

Giraffes are savanna mammals. They can grow up to 19 feet (5.8 m) tall. Giraffes use their height to reach tree leaves. But when they bend down to drink, they can be attacked. Giraffes can go days without drinking. This helps them avoid predators.

Lions

Lions are savanna predators. Their brownish color is like the color of savanna grasses. They blend in to hunt prey.

FUN FACT!

The lion is sometimes called the king of the jungle. But lions actually live in savannas.

Lions hunt zebras, antelope, giraffes, and other large animals.

Prairie Rattlesnakes

The prairie rattlesnake hunts grassland animals such as prairie dogs and mice. Rattlesnakes get their names from the rattles on their tails. When they are scared, they shake their tails to make a noise.

When a rattlesnake shakes the end of its tail, loose, hollow scales hit each other, making a rattling sound.

Rattlesnakes have two fangs, one on either side of the upper jaw.

Venom

These snakes are venomous. They bite animals such as mice, birds, and prairie dogs. The snake's venom, or poison, makes its prey weak. Then the rattlesnake eats it.

Grasshoppers rub their legs against their wings to make a buzzing sound.

Grasshoppers

Many grasshoppers live in grasslands. These insects have strong back legs for jumping. Grasshoppers live among and eat prairie grasses.

Birds

Many prairie songbirds have small feet. This helps them perch on tall grass or on twigs. Some birds, such as rock wrens, get most of the water they need from eating insects.

Dickcissels
live in dense
grasslands.

Controlled burns in grasslands keep trees and other plants from taking over.

Protecting Grasslands

The world's grasslands are smaller than they used to be. Grassland soil is good for farming. People replace grasslands with farms and towns. But this destroys wildlife homes. Some people are regrowing prairies.

Savanna Growth

Savannas have similar threats. Invasive species threaten savannas. These are species that do not come from savannas and take over the area. Controlled burns kill these plants. They let native plants grow.

Savanna Seasons

A savanna can look dead in its dry season. But when the rainy season comes, the savanna becomes green.

DRY SEASON

RAINY SEASON

Poaching

Wildlife poaching is a big problem in African savannas. The savanna is home to elephants, zebras, rhinoceroses, and more. People hunt African savanna wildlife. They kill some animals for sport.

Some artists carve ivory, which comes from tusks. Ivory sales are banned in many places.

Elephants are poached for their ivory tusks.

Poaching Laws

African governments made laws to stop these killings. People who illegally kill animals face punishment. This makes poaching less common. It protects the animals.

It can be hard to tell from the surface, but the ocean is full of life.

What Are Marine Biomes?

The ocean covers 70 percent of Earth. This forms the saltwater marine biome. It has different zones. There is deep and shallow ocean. There is cold and warm water.

Ocean Life

The ocean has more life than anywhere else on Earth. Most of this life is near coasts. But the deep ocean has amazing life too.

FUN FACT!

Humans have explored less than 10 percent of the ocean. There may be many unknown life-forms.

There are seven sea turtle species.

Plants

The ocean can be a tough place for plants. Plants need light, and deep water is dark. Waves make it hard for plants to stay rooted in the seafloor. There are some ocean plants. Seagrasses are an example.

Marine animals need ocean plants for food and shelter.

Kelps

There is also plant-like life. Kelps are a type of algae called seaweed. They are a life-form that is not plant or animal. Kelps grow in long strands. These strands are found in cold, shallow water. Kelps grow tall very quickly.

Some types of kelps can grow more than 100 feet (30 m) tall.

Shelter

Groups of kelps are called forests. These forests are a shelter for ocean animals. Kelps are food for small animals such as crabs.

Phytoplankton

Phytoplankton are very small life-forms. They are not plants or animals. But like plants, they make food from sunlight. Phytoplankton float on the ocean surface. They have shells to protect them. These creatures are an important ocean food source. Many small animals eat them.

Phytoplankton are so small people need microscopes to see them.

Marine Animals

The ocean is a very big place. Earth's biggest animals live there. Other ocean animals find unique ways to protect themselves. And deep ocean animals live and hunt in the dark.

Bigeye trevally fish swim in large groups called schools.

Blue Whales

Blue whales are Earth's largest animal. They can grow up to 100 feet (30 m) long. A blue whale can weigh 150 tons (140 metric tons). It lives in oceans around the world.

Whale Sounds

Blue whales often travel alone. They use sounds to talk to other whales. Blue whales can hear each other across very long distances. A blue whale's call can travel as far as 1,000 miles (1,600 km). This is how whales find each other.

Whale Size

Blue whales can be more than twice as long as a school bus.

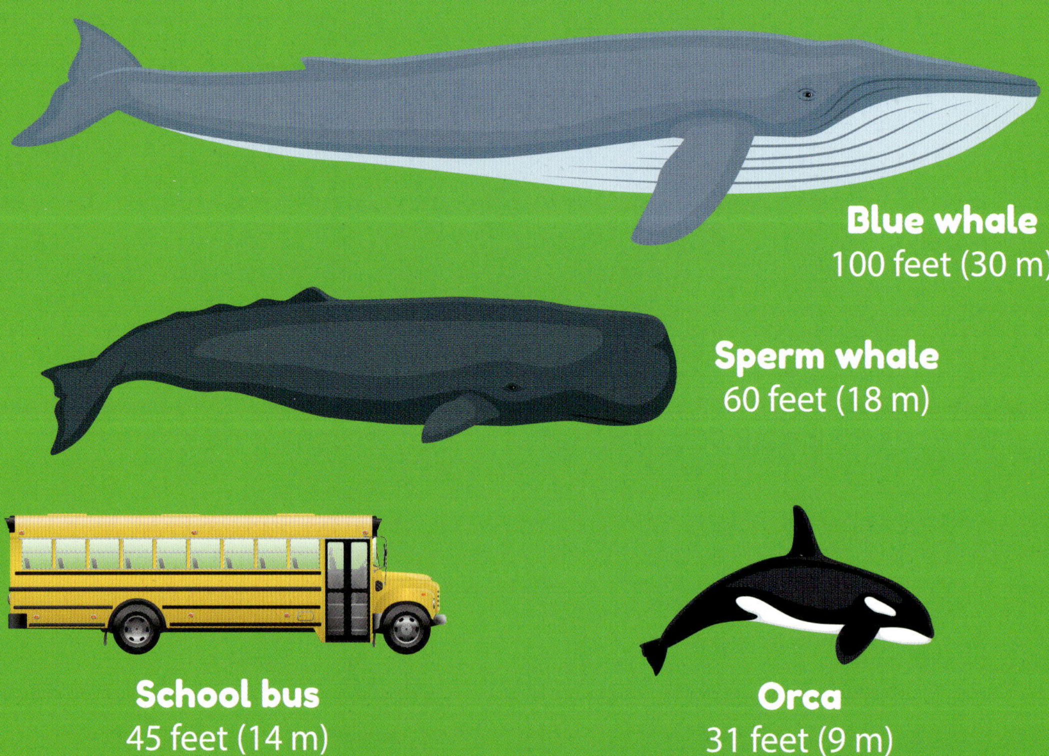

Sharks

Sharks can be big or small. The world's biggest fish is the whale shark. One fearsome shark is the great white. It can grow up to 20 feet (6 m) long. Great whites' bodies are smooth. They are narrow at the front and back. This helps them swim fast when they hunt.

Great white sharks sometimes leap out of the water to catch prey.

Krill

There are tiny ocean animals. Krill look like small shrimp. They live in large groups in the open sea. Many animals eat krill.

A krill's gills are on its front legs.

Fish can take shelter in coral reefs.

Corals

Corals are part of the marine biome. They live on the ocean floor. They group together. Some make skeletons that look like rocks. When some corals die, new ones grow on top of them. This makes coral reefs. Many sea animals live in coral reefs.

Great Barrier Reef

The world's biggest coral reef is the Great Barrier Reef. It lies off the Australian coast. It is 1,250 miles (2,000 km) long.

Cephalopods

Cephalopods live all around Earth's oceans. These are octopuses, squid, and cuttlefish. These animals have soft bodies. This helps them squeeze into tight spaces such as those in coral reefs.

Nautilus

Another type of cephalopod is the nautilus. This animal has a spiral shell.

There are more than 300 species of squid.

An octopus can have more than 2,200 suckers on its eight arms.

Octopuses

Some octopuses are very intelligent. They collect shells to make shelter. This helps them hide on the ocean floor.

FUN FACT!

Oysters are related to clams. Oysters make pearls when small objects, such as grains of sand, get inside their shells.

The prickly cockle is a type of sea clam. It uses a muscle called a foot to move.

Shells

Bivalve mollusks are animals that make their own shells. Clams and oysters are two types. These animals have soft, boneless bodies. They make shells to protect themselves.

Seahorses

Seahorses are small fish. They have horse-shaped heads and curly tails. A fin on this animal's back helps it swim. Male seahorses get pregnant instead of females. The female seahorse gives her eggs to the male. He carries the eggs and gives birth.

Seahorses are slow swimmers. Some can go only 4.9 feet (1.5 m) per hour.

Glowing Animals

The bottom of the ocean is very dark. Some deep-sea animals make their own light. They are bioluminescent. This means their bodies glow. One example is the anglerfish. Its head has a rod that sticks out. At the end is a glowing ball. Animals swim toward the light. Then the anglerfish eats them.

There are several species of anglerfish. One is the double anglerfish.

Corals bleach, or turn white, when waters become too warm or if they get stressed in other ways.

Protecting Marine Biomes

Climate change is dangerous for marine biomes. The ocean is getting warmer. Some species, such as corals, can die if the water stays too warm for too long. Scientists are trying to help coral reefs. They study how to help reefs grow back.

Anyone can clean up trash at a beach to help protect the ocean from pollution.

Pollution

Trash pollution is also a problem. There is a lot of garbage in the ocean. Ocean currents cause garbage to collect in patches. The biggest is called the Great Pacific Garbage Patch. This patch is twice the size of Texas.

Cleaning Up

Garbage hurts ocean life. Animals eat garbage by accident. It can trap them. People are working to clean up garbage. An organization called The Ocean Cleanup made a special U-shaped barrier. It helps catch plastic.

The Ocean Cleanup developed the barrier system under the leadership of Boyan Slat.

What Is Tundra?

Tundra is in places too cold for trees to grow. Arctic tundra is in the Arctic. This is the far north part of the world. The Arctic is a cold, harsh place.

The Nenets people have lived in the Russian tundra on the Yamal Peninsula for at least 1,000 years.

Alpine tundra starts at about 11,000 feet (3,400 m) above sea level.

Alpine Tundra

South of the Arctic, mountaintops also tend to be cold. If they are cold enough, trees will not grow on them. The place where trees stop growing because of cold is called the tree line. Alpine tundra is above the tree line on mountains.

FUN FACT!

Tundra comes the word *tūndar* in a Sámi language. It means "treeless hill."

Permafrost can be more than 1 mile (1.6 km) deep.

Soil

Tundra covers about 10 percent of the world. It is hard for life to grow there. Tundra soil is often frozen. Some soil is frozen year-round. This is called permafrost.

Plants

The tundra has a short growing season. It is hard for plants to grow in frozen soil. The soil that does thaw is low in nutrients. So the plants that grow there are short and hardy. They grow in groups to shelter each other from wind.

The tufted saxifrage is a short Arctic and alpine herb with white flowers.

Mosses

Mosses are plants suited to the harsh tundra. They don't have flowers or roots. Mosses hold on to surfaces instead. They can get water from the air. They can live even with frozen soil.

Woolly fringe-moss is one type of Arctic moss.

Shrubs

There are short shrubs in the Arctic tundra. One is the dwarf shrub. It doesn't grow taller than 16 inches (41 cm). It also grows in alpine tundra. Short plants are good at resisting wind.

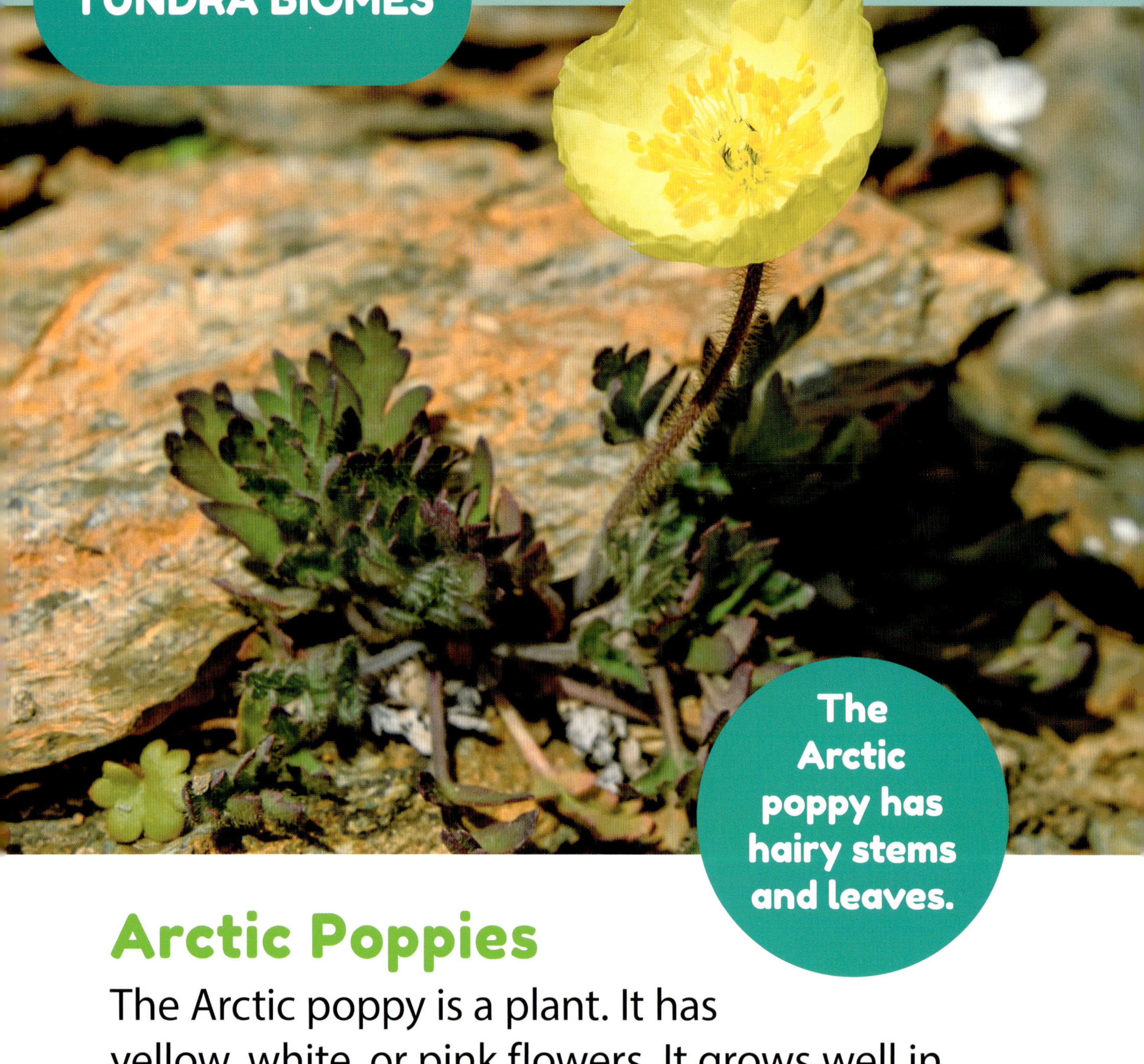

The Arctic poppy has hairy stems and leaves.

Arctic Poppies

The Arctic poppy is a plant. It has yellow, white, or pink flowers. It grows well in cold, dry soil. Arctic poppies live in Arctic and alpine tundra. They are about 6 inches (15 cm) tall.

Lichens

Some tundra life-forms are not animals or plants. Lichens do not have roots or stems. They can grow without soil.

Reindeer lichen is one type of lichen that caribou in the tundra eat.

Lichen Parts

Lichens are a mix of fungi and algae or bacteria. The fungi give the algae or bacteria shelter. The algae or bacteria give the fungi food. Lichens are food for large mammals such as caribou.

Inside a Lichen

A lichen has an outer casing called a cortex. Inside the cortex is a layer of algae or bacteria and a layer of fungi.

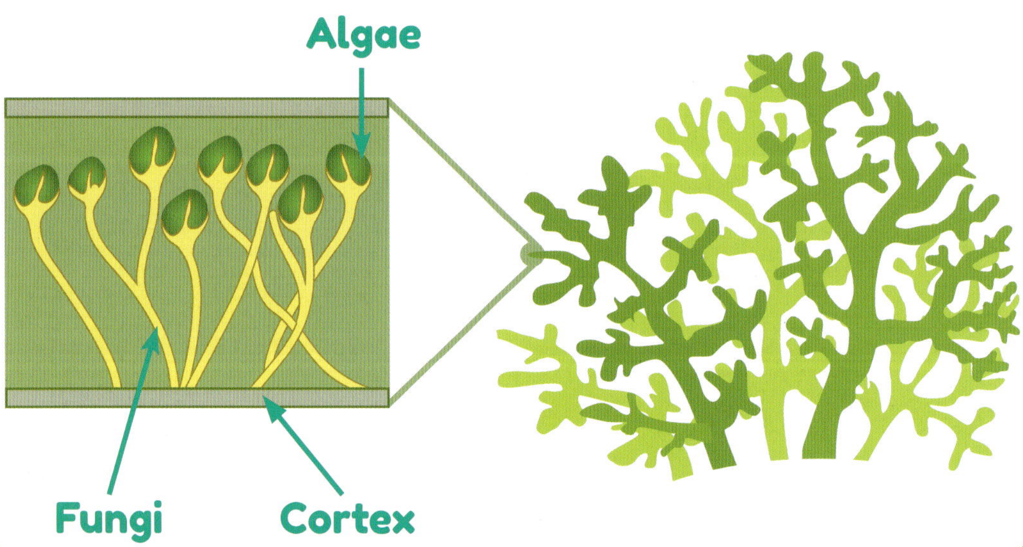

Tundra Animals

The tundra is snowy. In winter, it is very white. Some tundra animals are white as well. Their color helps them blend in. This can help them hunt or hide.

Arctic foxes are white in winter and brown in summer.

Animals Keeping Warm

Tundra animals must keep warm. Arctic foxes and polar bears have thick fur. Arctic foxes have short ears and snouts. This is so that less heat escapes from their heads. Polar bears have a lot of body fat. The fat keeps them warm.

Arctic Wolves

Arctic wolves are tundra predators. They have thick white fur. They feed on Arctic hares. Hares are animals similar to rabbits. Wolves also hunt caribou.

FUN FACT!

Caribou sometimes combine herds. A super-herd can have up to 500,000 caribou.

One reason Arctic wolves howl is to find other members of their pack.

Caribou

Caribou are part of the deer family. Caribou have coats with two layers. These layers help them survive frozen weather. Caribou graze on plants and lichens. Their large antlers help them find food. They push the snow away with their antlers. Male caribou also fight by locking antlers.

Two Names

Caribou and reindeer are the same animal with two names. Those in Europe and Asia are called reindeer. Those in North America are called caribou.

A male caribou, *pictured*, is called a bull. A female is a cow.

Birds

The snowy owl is a mostly white Arctic bird. Tundra swans are also white. They make their nests in the far north in summer.

Rock Ptarmigan

The rock ptarmigan is about 1 foot (30 cm) tall. These birds look like chickens. They are brown in summer. They blend in with the rocky ground. They turn white in winter. Then they match the snow.

Insects

The tundra is too cold for reptiles. There are few types of insects in cold places. But there are many mosquitoes.

Mosquitoes

Mosquitoes live all over the world. The Arctic mosquito is a large mosquito. It often travels in swarms. It stays frozen as an egg. Then it hatches in the springtime.

Protecting the Tundra

Earth's climate is getting warmer. Even the Arctic is getting hotter. In hotter weather, ice melts. Animals such as polar bears live and hunt on ice. Without it, their hunting grounds shrink. They are more likely to starve.

Unlike other mosquitoes, Arctic mosquitoes do not carry diseases that can pass to humans.

Polar bears wait on the ice for seals to come up to breathe.

Red foxes are moving into Arctic fox territory because of warming.

Warming Risks

Warming lets shrubs grow farther north. They take the place of lichens. Most shrubs do not produce food during winter. But lichens stay alive during winter.

Slowing the Warming

Scientists are working to slow climate change. One way is by reducing the use of fossil fuels such as gas and coal. Burning these fuels makes the planet warmer.

Glaciers

Glaciers are huge, constantly moving bodies of ice. They hold most of the world's fresh water.

Cars and other machines that use fossil fuels release greenhouse gases into the air.

GLOSSARY

adapted
Changed as a species in a way that helped the species survive in certain conditions.

amphibian
An animal that can live in water and on land.

bacteria
Tiny, one-celled organisms that live in water, soil, and the bodies of animals or plants.

climate
The usual weather patterns in a region over a long period of time.

current
The regular movement of water or air in a certain direction.

fungi
Types of life-forms that are neither plants nor animals and consume dead matter.

mammal
An animal that has hair and makes milk. Humans are mammals.

predator
An animal that hunts and eats other animals.

prey
An animal that is hunted and eaten by other animals.

protein
A substance that animals need to live and grow.

reptile
An animal with scales or plates that uses its surroundings to warm up or cool down.

species
A group of animals or plants that share characteristics and can mate and produce offspring.

TO LEARN MORE

More Books to Read

Habitats of the World. DK, 2023.

Mooney, Carla. *Life Science*. Abdo, 2025.

Silen, Andrea. *Rainforests.* National Geographic Kids, 2020.

Online Resources

Booklinks
NONFICTION NETWORK
FREE! ONLINE NONFICTION RESOURCES

To learn more about biomes, please visit **abdobooklinks.com** or scan this QR code. These links are routinely monitored and updated to provide the most current information available.

INDEX

PHOTO CREDITS

Cover Photos: Shutterstock Images, front (cactus, coral reef), back (flower); Puttachat Kumkrong/ Shutterstock Images, front (ocean); Dirk Ercken/Shutterstock Images, front (frog)

Interior Photos: Shutterstock Images, 1, 3, 5, 6, 10, 12, 16, 20–21, 23, 24, 28 (rainforest), 28 (animals), 29, 33, 35, 42 (top), 43 (top), 43 (bottom), 44, 47 (middle left), 47 (middle right), 47 (bottom left), 47 (bottom right), 49, 53, 56, 57, 58 (top), 60, 63, 64, 67, 68, 71, 72, 74 (bottom), 80, 83 (left), 84, 85, 86, 88, 94 (whales), 94 (bus), 96, 97 (bottom), 98 (top), 98 (bottom), 101, 107, 113, 116 (left), 118 (top), 119, 123, 124, 125 (top), 125 (bottom); Sarawut Kundej/Shutterstock Images, 4; Emily Marie Wilson/Shutterstock Images, 7; Wojciech Dziadosz/ Shutterstock Images, 8; Red Line Editorial, 9, 114 (left); Scisetti Alfio/Shutterstock Images, 11; Arnold O. A. Pinto/Shutterstock Images, 13; Danny Smythe/Shutterstock Images, 14; Gerald Corsi/iStockphoto, 15; Eric Isselee/Shutterstock Images, 17 (top), 77; Karpenko Ilia/Shutterstock Images, 17 (bottom); Pascale Gueret/ Shutterstock Images, 18; Warren Metcalf/Shutterstock Images, 19; Linda J. Scher/Shutterstock Images, 21; Filip Fuxa/Shutterstock Images, 22; CFOTO/Future Publishing/Getty Images, 25 (top); Raul Almu/Shutterstock Images, 25 (bottom); Dietrich Leppert/Shutterstock Images, 26; George Trumpeter/Shutterstock Images, 27; Pierre Leclerc/Shutterstock Images, 30; Vladimir Volodin/Shutterstock Images, 31 (top); Martin Poirier/ Shutterstock Images, 31 (bottom); Vova Shevchuk/Shutterstock Images, 32; Cavan Images/Shutterstock Images, 34, 122; Anton Starikov/Shutterstock Images, 36 (top); Nataly Studio/Shutterstock Images, 36 (bottom); Menno Schaefer/Shutterstock Images, 37; Jack Bell Photography/Shutterstock Images, 38; Hung Chung Chih/Shutterstock Images, 39; Passakorn Umpornmaha/Shutterstock Images, 40; Gudkov Andrey/ Shutterstock Images, 41; Tanya Leanovich/Shutterstock Images, 42 (bottom); Jacob Lund/Shutterstock Images, 45; Romiana Lee/Shutterstock Images, 46; Simakova Mariia/Shutterstock Images, 47 (top); Andrey Ch/Shutterstock Images, 48; Kristi Blokhin/Shutterstock Images, 50; Studio 888/Shutterstock Images, 51; Martin Prochazkacz/Shutterstock Images, 52, 90; Lotus Studio/Shutterstock Images, 54; Paco Como/ Shutterstock Images, 55; Profi Trollka/Shutterstock Images, 58 (bottom), 74 (top); Danita Delimont/ Shutterstock Images, 59; Ilias Strachinis/Shutterstock Images, 60–61; Jordan Feeg/Shutterstock Images, 62; James Wakibia/SOPA Images/LightRocket/Getty Images, 65; Ricardo Reitmeyer/Shutterstock Images, 66; Tom Tietz/Shutterstock Images, 69; Wayan Sumatika/Shutterstock Images, 70; Dudarev Mikhail/Shutterstock Images, 73; Zoltan Tarlacz/Shutterstock Images, 75 (top); Himawan Rush/Shutterstock Images, 75 (bottom); Andrzej Kubik/Shutterstock Images, 76; Harris Motion Photo/Shutterstock Images, 78; Joe McDonald/ Shutterstock Images, 79; Stephen A. Waycott/Shutterstock Images, 81; B. Gardner/Shutterstock Images, 82; Art Konovalov/Shutterstock Images, 83 (right); Rich Carey/Shutterstock Images, 87; Zhane Luk/Shutterstock Images, 89; Ekky Ilham/Shutterstock Images, 91; Leonardo Gonzalez/Shutterstock Images, 92; Mike Johnson/ Blue Planet Archive, 93; Sergey Uryadnikov/Shutterstock Images, 95; Joe Belanger/Shutterstock Images, 97 (top); Pan Demin/Shutterstock Images, 99; Picture Partners Holland/Science Source, 100; Doug Perrine/ Blue Planet Archive, 102; Jon Milnes/Shutterstock Images, 103; Susan Dabritz/Blue Planet Archive, 104; The Ocean Cleanup, 105; Evgenii Mitroshin/Shutterstock Images, 106; Kerstin Langenberger/imageBROKER.com GmbH & Co. KG/Alamy, 108; Vladimir Melnik/Shutterstock Images, 109; Wolfgang Kaehler/LightRocket/Getty Images, 110; Michal Hykel/Shutterstock Images, 111; Iri Sha/Shutterstock Images, 112; Lis Wilks/Shutterstock Images, 114 (right); Ilya Akinshin/Shutterstock Images, 115; Ondrej Prosicky/Shutterstock Images, 116 (right); Timothy Stringer/Shutterstock Images, 117; Jeff McGraw/Shutterstock Images, 118 (bottom); Rock Ptarmigan/ Shutterstock Images, 120; Galaxiid/Alamy, 121